Castle adventure

A playscript
adapted from a story by
Roderick Hunt

by Jacquie Buttriss and Ann Callander

Characters

Narrator 1

Narrator 2

Gran

Frog-King

Chip

Biff

This play has six speaking parts so that it can be read aloud in small groups. Sound effects can be added by children when they are familiar with the playscript but they have not been written in.
The story in this play follows on from 'Gran'.

Gran
Narrator 1
Biff
Chip
Frog-King
Narrator 2

Scene 1

Narrator 1 Scene 1 'A new adventure'
The magic key was glowing.
The magic took Gran and the
children to a castle.

Scene 2

Narrator 2   Scene 2   'A room in the castle' The magic took Gran and the children inside the castle.

Chip   I don't like this castle.

Narrator 1   A frog was in the room.

Biff Look at that frog.

Frog-King I am a king.
I am the king of this castle.

Chip You look like a frog.

Frog-King   Three witches live in this castle.

Gran   I don't like witches.

Frog-King   They turned me into a frog.
Help me.

Scene 3

Narrator 1 Scene 3 'The black witch'
A witch was coming.

Frog-King Look out!

Narrator 2 The door opened.

Frog-King It's the black witch.

Gran I don't like witches.

Narrator 1 Gran pushed the witch.

Biff Good old Gran.

9

Frog-King Get the keys.

Narrator 2 Chip took the witch's keys.

Chip Come on.

Narrator 1 They ran out of the room.

Biff Lock the door, Chip.

Narrator 2 Chip locked the door.
The witch couldn't get out.

Scene 4

Narrator 1 Scene 4   'The red witch'
Everyone ran.

Chip Look out!

Biff A witch is coming.

Frog-King It's the red witch.

Gran I don't like witches.

Narrator 2 Gran put a net over the witch.

Chip Look at the witch.

Biff Good old Gran.

Narrator 1 The witch couldn't get out.

Scene 5

Narrator 2 Scene 5   'The green witch'
Gran went to the green witch.

Gran I don't like witches.

Narrator 1 The witch looked frightened.

Gran I don't like nasty witches.

Chip   Come on, Gran.

Frog-King Get the witch.

Narrator 2 Gran threw the witch on the floor.

Biff   Good old Gran.

Scene 6

Narrator 1   Scene 6   'The witches' book'
The frog-king jumped on the table.

Frog-King   Help me.

Narrator 2   Biff and Gran looked in the witches' book.

Chip Look at the frog.

Narrator 1 The frog turned into the king.

Gran It's magic.

Biff Good old Gran.

Frog-King Turn the witches into frogs.

Narrator 2 Gran turned the witches into frogs.

Gran I don't like witches.

Narrator 1 Gran put the book on the fire.

20

Scene 7

Narrator 2   Scene 7   'The party'
The king had a party.

Frog-King   Come to my party.

Gran   What a good party.

Chip   Good old Gran.

Scene 8

Narrator 1 Scene 8 'The adventure ends'

Narrator 2 The magic key was glowing.

Gran Look at the key.

Biff It's time to go.

Frog-King Goodbye.

Narrator 1 The magic took them back to Biff's room.

Narrator 2 They fell on to Biff's bed.

Chip Oh no!

Gran What an adventure!

The end

Printed in Hong Kong